What
Is
Funny?

VLB
Veronica Lane Books

What Is Funny?

By Etan Boritzer   Illustrated by Jeff Day

2nd Printing 2006

 Veronica Lane Books

www.veronicalanebooks.com   e-mail: books@veronicalanebooks.com
2554 Lincoln Blvd., Ste 142,
Los Angeles, CA 90291 USA
Tel: (800) 651-1001

Library of Congress Cataloging-In-Publication Data
        Boritzer, Etan, 1950-
        What Is Funny?

Library of Congress Catalog Card Number 2004090426

Summary: The author presents various points of view on sensitivity and awareness in children's
humor.

ISBN 0-9637597-8-7 (bound) ISBN 0-9637597-9-5 (pbk)

1. Psychology-Wit and Humor-152.43
     I. Day, Jeff, 1947-   I. Title

... to the children
of the world...

What is funny?

If you see a bunch of clowns at the circus
slip on a bunch of banana peels
and flop all around the floor,
is that funny?

If you see two clowns at the circus
run at each other real fast
and bump their heads together real hard,
is that funny?

If one clown squirts water
out of a flower on his coat
into another clown's face,
is that funny?

If I slip on a banana peal,
is that funny?
If you slip on a banana peal,
is that funny?
What is Funny?

We say something is funny
when we laugh,
but is everything we laugh at funny?

If your Dad tickles
the bottoms of your feet,
or your belly,
or under your arms,
you laugh, don't you?

But what if
someone tickles you for a long time,
and doesn't stop?
Do you still laugh?
Is that funny?

Can you tickle yourself
and laugh?
Go ahead and try it!
Did you laugh?

What makes us laugh one time
and not laugh the next time?

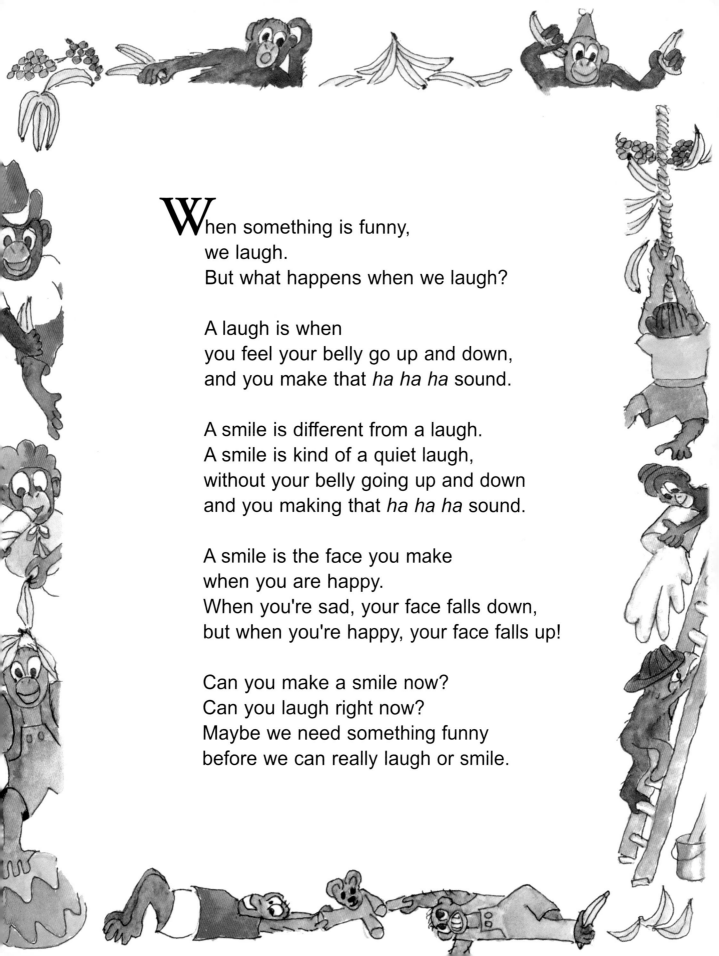

When something is funny,
we laugh.
But what happens when we laugh?

A laugh is when
you feel your belly go up and down,
and you make that *ha ha ha* sound.

A smile is different from a laugh.
A smile is kind of a quiet laugh,
without your belly going up and down
and you making that *ha ha ha* sound.

A smile is the face you make
when you are happy.
When you're sad, your face falls down,
but when you're happy, your face falls up!

Can you make a smile now?
Can you laugh right now?
Maybe we need something funny
before we can really laugh or smile.

When did we learn to laugh?
I don't remember learning to laugh,
do you?

Maybe when we were babies,
our Mom or Dad,
or our Grandpa or Grandma,
smiled at us,
and made some funny sounds
like *googoo gaagaa*.
Maybe that's when we started to smile.
Maybe then they tickled us a little
and that made us laugh.

Or maybe when you were a baby,
your older sister or brother
made some silly faces at you
like buggin' out their eyes
or bouncing their heads from side to side-
and that's when you started to laugh,
do you think?

What is Funny?

Some animals are funny.
Ducks are funny, aren't they?
Look at the way they walk
from side to side,
the funny way they talk-
quackquackquackquackquack!
Ducks even have funny faces,
don't they?

If you and your friend
pretend you're ducks,
and you both walk like ducks,
and make funny faces like ducks,
and *quackquackquackquackquack*
like ducks--
that's kind of funny
and makes you laugh,
doesn't it?

I wonder why
we think ducks are funny,
don't you?

Are all animals funny?

If you and your friend act like lions
and roar real loud
and raise your hands up and down
like you're going to scratch somebody,
is that funny?

If your baby sister
sees you acting like lions,
and hears you roaring like lions,
and she gets scared
and starts crying,
is that funny?

Piggies are kind of funny,
but is a snake funny?
Ostriches make me laugh,
but an eagle doesn't.

How can you tell which animals are funny
and which animals are not funny?
Why do we laugh at ducks,
but not at lions?

How do we know what is funny,
and what is not funny?

Giraffes look funny
because they have long necks,
but if you see a girl with a long neck,
is that funny?

A hippopotamus looks funny
because it is big and round,
but if you see a boy
who is big and round,
is that funny?

Chickens sound funny
because they have very high voices,
but if a boy has a high voice,
is that funny?

Maybe we all have something
that looks or sounds funny
to somebody else.
Is making fun of somebody else funny?
Is it OK to laugh at somebody?

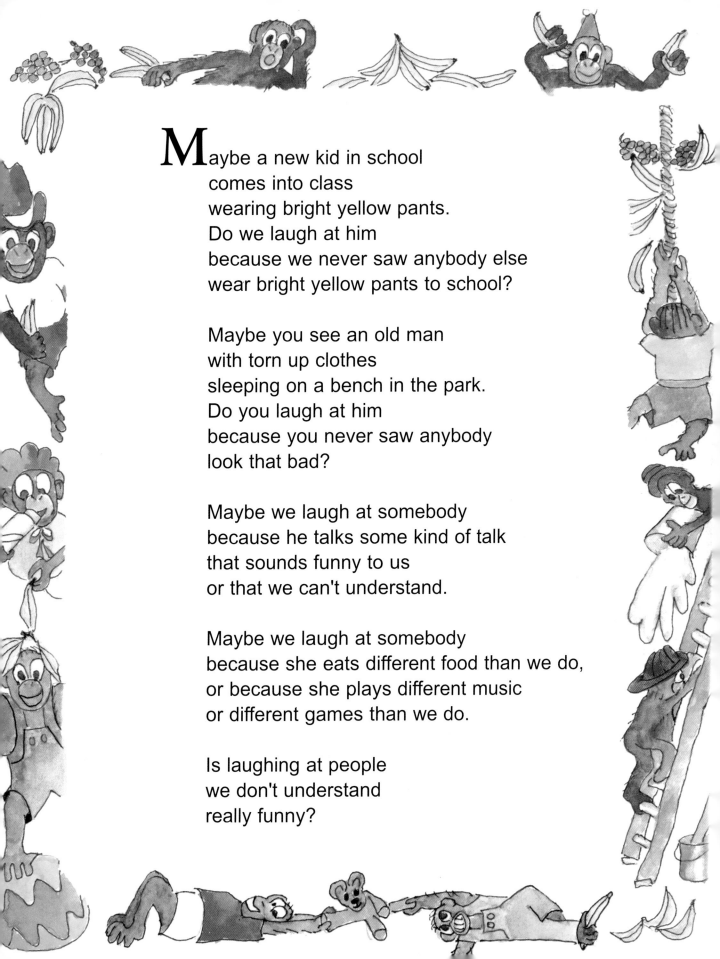

Maybe a new kid in school
comes into class
wearing bright yellow pants.
Do we laugh at him
because we never saw anybody else
wear bright yellow pants to school?

Maybe you see an old man
with torn up clothes
sleeping on a bench in the park.
Do you laugh at him
because you never saw anybody
look that bad?

Maybe we laugh at somebody
because he talks some kind of talk
that sounds funny to us
or that we can't understand.

Maybe we laugh at somebody
because she eats different food than we do,
or because she plays different music
or different games than we do.

Is laughing at people
we don't understand
really funny?

Do animals laugh,
or do only people laugh?

Animals can be happy,
like when a doggie is wagging his tail
and jumping around.

Animals can be sad too,
like when you go to school
and your doggie misses you.

But do animals laugh?
Do animals think things are funny?
(Do animals think?)
Do animals laugh at other animals?

Sometimes it looks like monkeys laugh,
and sometimes it sounds
like seals are laughing.

Do flowers or bugs laugh?
Does the sun or the moon laugh?
Is the wind laughing?

Hey, if you think about it,
we're all kind of like animals—
only we walk around on two legs,
and we don't have any feathers or fur!

But maybe we're the only animals
who think things are funny.
Maybe we're the only animals
who can really laugh!

Maybe animals think we look funny.
Maybe they think we make funny sounds,
or that we smell funny--
Maybe the animals
are really laughing at us!

Whoops!

Maybe something is funny
when it's kind of a surprise!

(A surprise is something
that you don't know about ahead of time,
like a surprise birthday party!)

If your Mom tells you
to go and brush your teeth,
and instead, you take your toothbrush
and start to brush your ear
while your baby brother is watching
and laughing—
that may be a funny surprise.

But if you poke the inside of your ear too hard,
while you're brushing your ear—
Ouch! That could hurt!
(And not be a funny surprise.)

Then, what if your baby brother
laughs at you while you're crying
because your ear hurts so much,
because you poked it so hard by surprise-
is that funny?

Sometimes a kid in school
thinks it's funny to make faces
when the teacher's back is turned.

Sometimes we think it's funny
to do something we're not supposed to do,
like a secret thing.

(A secret is something
that you don't tell anybody else about.)

Are secret things funny?
Maybe.

But what if your friend has a secret
or knows something
that she's afraid to tell anybody?
How can that be funny?

Really funny things
don't hurt anybody--
and we don't have to keep them a secret.

Did you ever laugh—
just because?

Did you ever run down the beach
with your friends, or your doggie,
in your bare feet,
in and out of the water,
in the hot sunshine,
and laugh—
just because?

Sometimes we laugh
just because we feel like it.

Sometimes we laugh
just because we're happy
and it feels good to laugh.

Sometimes we laugh
not because anything is funny—
just because.

Can you laugh at yourself?

Maybe once you were running real fast
down a hallway, and you couldn't stop,
and you bumped your knee real hard
into a door, and you fell down,
and your knee hurt real bad,
and your friend saw you,
so you tried not to cry!

Then maybe your friend started to laugh.
At first you were angry at your friend
for making fun of you,
but then your friend showed you
how funny you looked
when you ran real fast into that door
and bumped your knee
and fell down.

At first you didn't want to laugh,
but then, maybe you had to laugh,
because, well…it did look kind of funny...
And you did feel a little better
after you started to laugh, remember?

Sometimes laughing is better than crying.
Sometimes if we can laugh at ourselves
even a little bit,
we can feel a whole lot better.

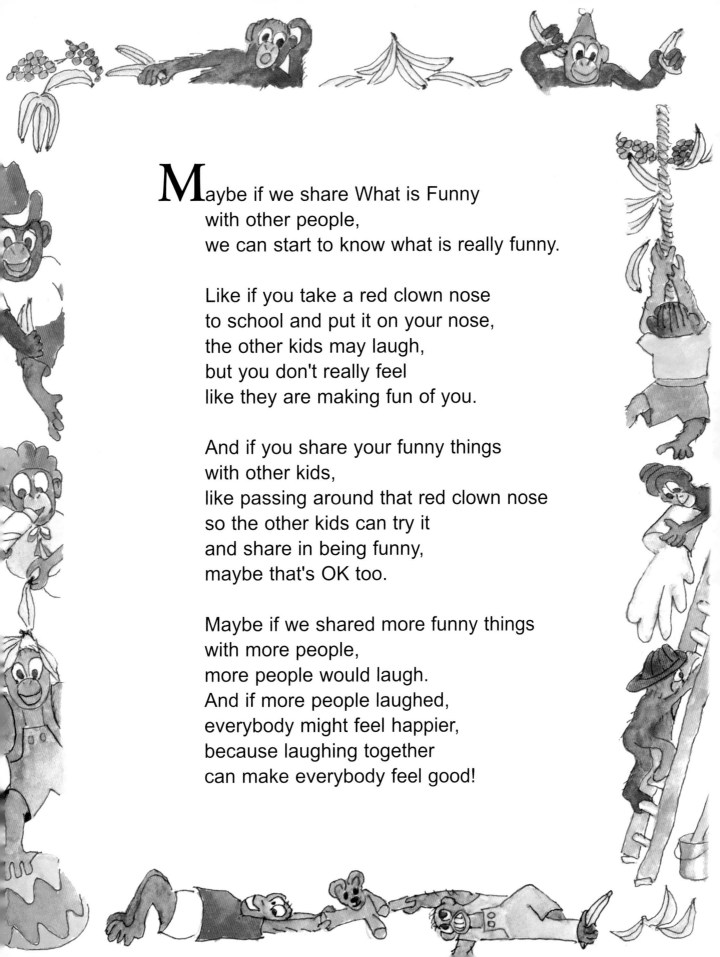

Maybe if we share What is Funny
with other people,
we can start to know what is really funny.

Like if you take a red clown nose
to school and put it on your nose,
the other kids may laugh,
but you don't really feel
like they are making fun of you.

And if you share your funny things
with other kids,
like passing around that red clown nose
so the other kids can try it
and share in being funny,
maybe that's OK too.

Maybe if we shared more funny things
with more people,
more people would laugh.
And if more people laughed,
everybody might feel happier,
because laughing together
can make everybody feel good!

So, if we really want to know
What is Funny,
maybe we can start
by remembering that What is Funny
is something we can share
with a lot of other people.

Something is not funny
if it hurts somebody else
or if it cannot be shared
with other people.

If we can share
what is really funny
with a lot of other people,
maybe more people
will start to laugh together.

And maybe if we all laugh together
maybe sad people won't feel so sad,
and sick people won't feel so sick!

So maybe we should all keep thinking
about What is Funny?
so that we can all laugh more
and feel a little better
and feel a little happier-
starting right now!